JUL 1 7 2014

P9-DIJ-477

MAKE IT MINE

Kid Style

ROCKIN' BEDROOMS FOR YOU!

by Megan Cooley Peterson

Consulting editor: Gail Saunders-Smith, PhD

CAPSTONE PRESS
a capstone imprint

Pebble Plus is published by Capstone Press,
1710 Roe Crest Drive, North Mankato, Minnesota 56003
www.capstonepub.com

Library of Congress Cataloging-in-Publication Data
Peterson, Megan Cooley,
Kid style. Rockin' bedrooms for you! / by Megan Cooley Peterson.
pages cm.—(Pebble plus. Make it mine)
Summary: "Full-color photographs and simple text provide easy ways to
personalize a child's bedroom"—Provided by publisher.
Audience: 5-8.
Audience: Grade K to 3.
Includes bibliographical references.
ISBN 978-1-4765-3970-6 (library binding)
ISBN 978-1-4765-6033-5 (ebook pdf)
1. House furnishings—Juvenile literature. 2. Decoration and ornament—Juvenile
literature. 3. Bedrooms—Juvenile literature. 4. Handicraft—Juvenile literature. 5.
Interior decoration—Juvenile literature. 6. Childrens' rooms—Juvenile literature.
I. Title. II. Title: Rockin' bedrooms for you! III. Title: Rocking bedrooms for you!
TX315.P48 2014
747.7'7—dc23   2013035763

Editorial Credits
Jeni Wittrock, editor; Tracy Davies McCabe, designer; Svetlana Zhurkin,
media researcher; Jennifer Walker, production specialist; Sarah Schuette,
photo stylist; Marcy Morin, photo scheduler

Photo Credits
All photos by Capstone Studio/Karon Dubke

Printed in the United States of America in North Mankato, Minnesota.
092013   007775CGS14

TABLE OF CONTENTS

A Room of Your Own

Your bedroom is a space to dream and have fun. Kick back in a room as creative as you.

Many supplies for these projects can be found at home. The rest can be purchased at a craft store.

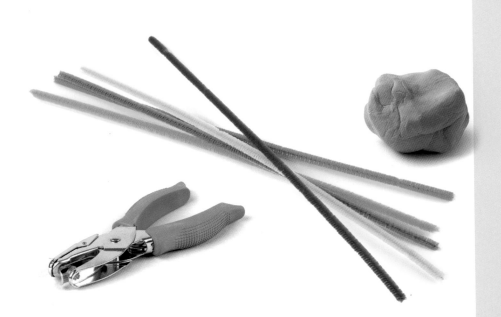

Basic Tools list:

- duct tape
- scissors
- craft foam
- hole punch
- ribbon
- fabric markers
- 3-D paint
- acrylic paint
- modeling clay
- chenille stems
- fabric
- decoupage glue

Light It Up

Flip the switch to

a stylish bedroom!

First ask an adult to remove

your light switch cover.

Paint squiggles and stripes on the cover. Add your name in funky lettering.

Mirror, Mirror

Free paint sample cards make a colorful border for your mirror. Cut out different shapes. Tape them to your mirror.

A Place for Pencils

Dress up a boring desk

with a splashy pencil holder.

Cover a can cooler with

stickers and colorful tape.

Do your homework in style!

13

Photo Holders

Say cheese! Turn old
binder clips into photo holders.
Wrap the clips with ribbons
and colorful tape.
Slip your photos into the clips.

Crafty Corkboard

Turn a corkboard into art. First dip old rubber stamps in paint. Stamp all over the corkboard. Wrap the frame in fun tape or stickers.

Keep Out!

Let the world know your bedroom belongs to you! To begin, mold modeling clay into the letters of your name. Let them dry.

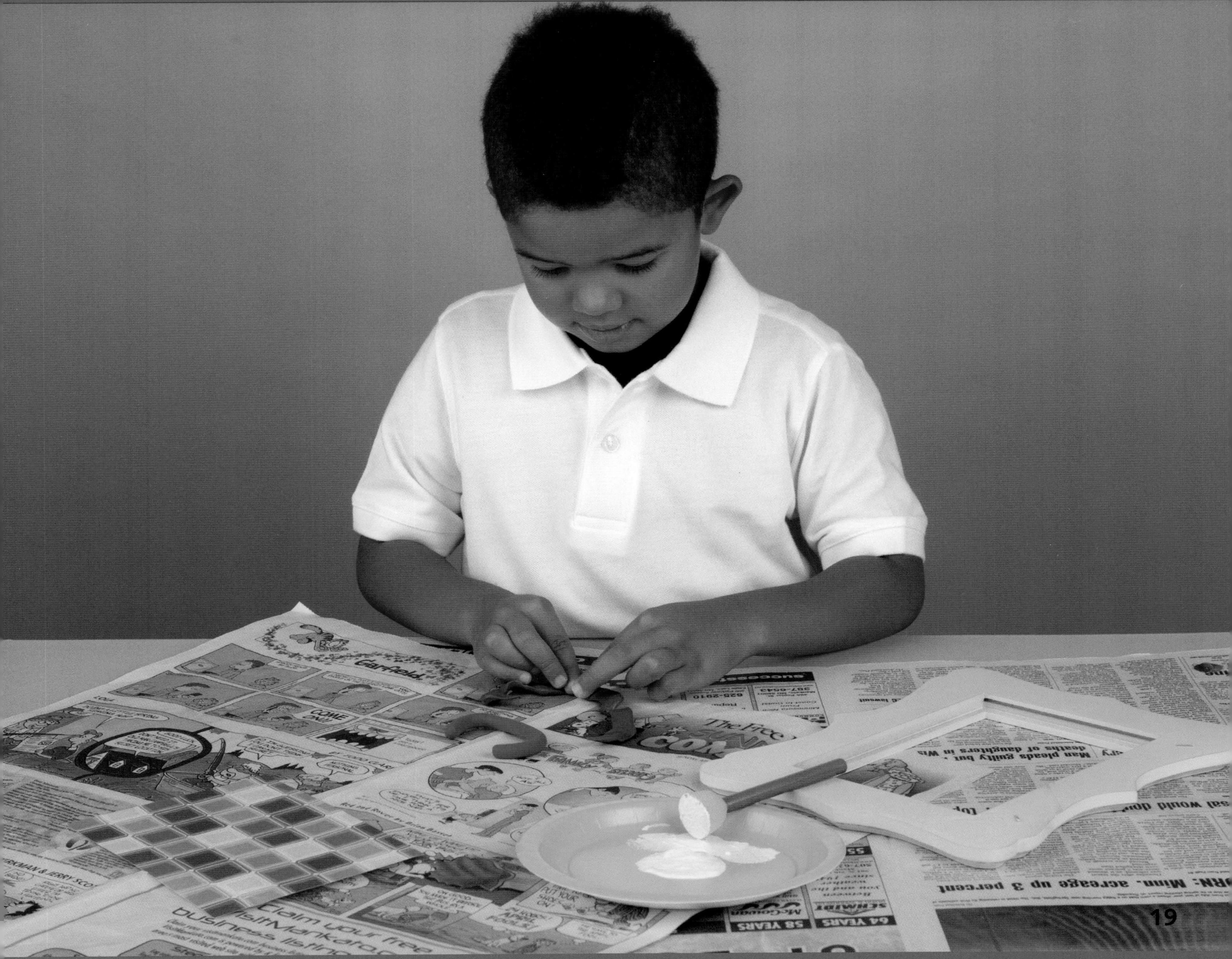

Garfield
COME ON!!

Paint an old picture frame. Paint the backing too if it is plain cardboard. Ask an adult to hot glue the letters inside the frame. Now hang it up!

Take It to the Next Level

Impress your friends with a one-of-a-kind pillowcase. Follow these steps or make your own pillowcase creation. Using your imagination is the best part!

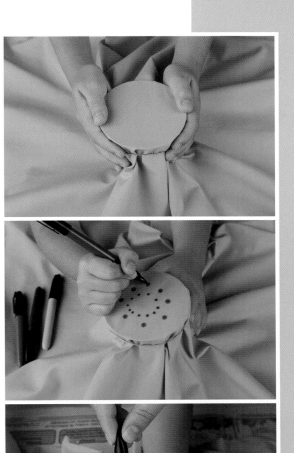

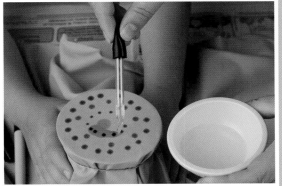

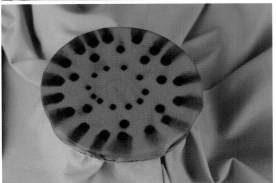

Step 1: Place a section of the pillowcase over a plastic cup. Secure the pillowcase to the cup with a rubber band.

Step 2: Using permanent markers, draw a designs or your name on the pillowcase. Repeat as needed.

Step 3: Ask an adult to drop rubbing alcohol onto your designs. The more drops you add, the more the colors will bleed. Let it dry overnight.

Step 4: Ask an adult to wash your pillowcase in cold water. Then slip it onto your pillow and enjoy!

Read More

Claybourne, Anna. *Bedroom Makeover.* Be Creative. Mankato, Minn.: Smart Apple Media, 2013.

Ross, Kathy. *Bedroom Makeover Crafts.* Girl Crafts. Minneapolis: Millbrook Press, 2009.

Sirrine, Carol. *Cool Crafts with Old Wrappers, Cans, and Bottles: Green Projects for Resourceful Kids.* Mankato, Minn.: Capstone Press, 2010.

Internet Sites

FactHound offers a safe, fun way to find Internet sites related to this book. All of the sites on FactHound have been researched by our staff.

Here's all you do:

Visit *www.facthound.com*

Type in this code: 9781476539706

Check out projects, games and lots more at
www.capstonekids.com

24

Word Count: 216
Grade: 1
Early-Intervention Level: 18